SECRETS
OF THE
ANIMAL WORLD

BUTTERFLIES
Magical Metamorphosis

956753

by Eulalia García
Illustrated by Gabriel Casadevall and Ali Garousi

Gareth Stevens Publishing
MILWAUKEE

For a free color catalog describing Gareth Stevens' list of high-quality books and
multimedia programs, call 1-800-542-2595 (USA) or 1-800-461-9120 (Canada).
Gareth Stevens Publishing's Fax: (414) 225-0377.
See our catalog, too, on the World Wide Web: http://gsinc.com

The editor would like to extend special thanks to Richard Sajdak, Milwaukee
County Zoo, Milwaukee, Wisconsin, for his kind and professional help with the
information in this book.

Library of Congress Cataloging-in-Publication Data

García, Eulalia.
    [Mariposa. English]
    Butterflies: magical metamorphosis / by Eulalia García; illustrated by Gabriel
Casadevall and Ali Garousi.
        p. cm. – (Secrets of the animal world.)
    Includes bibliographical references and index.
    Summary: Describes the life cycle, physical characteristics, behavior, and role in
pollination of butterflies.
    ISBN 0-8368-1540-8 (lib. bdg.)
    1. Butterflies–Juvenile literature. [1. Butterflies.] I. Casadevall, Gabriel, ill.
II. Garousi, Ali, ill. III. Title. IV. Series
QL544.2.G3713   1996
595.78'9–dc20   95-54163

This North American edition first published in 1996 by
Gareth Stevens Publishing
1555 North RiverCenter Drive, Suite 201
Milwaukee, Wisconsin 53212 USA

This U.S. edition © 1996 by Gareth Stevens, Inc. Created with original © 1993
Ediciones Este, S.A., Barcelona, Spain. Additional end matter © 1996 by Gareth
Stevens, Inc.

Series editor: Patricia Lantier-Sampon
Editorial assistants: Jamie Daniel, Diane Laska, Rita Reitci

Printed in the United States of America

1 2 3 4 5 6 7 8 9 99 98 97 96

CONTENTS

THE BUTTERFLY'S WORLD

Worldwide habitat

Butterflies are insects, and they are more numerous than any other insects except beetles. Butterflies belong to the scientific order Lepidoptera. They thrive in several areas of the world — in forests, jungles, swamps, and dry zones. Butterflies that live in different geographical regions look and behave differently from each other because each species adapts itself to its specific environment in order to grow and reproduce.

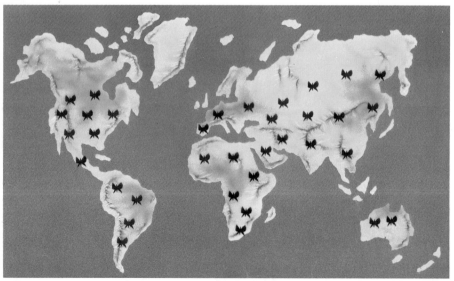

Butterflies are beautiful creatures; they also have many surprising qualities.

Butterflies live all over the world except in the coldest and hottest regions.

Four stages of growth

Butterflies are oviparous; they lay eggs that hatch outside the mother's body. But unlike other oviparous animals, such as birds and reptiles, butterfly babies are not fully formed when they emerge from the eggs. Like many other insects, butterflies have a complicated, but magical, pattern of development. They pass through four very different stages that produce major changes in the insect. These changes — which move from egg to larva (caterpillar) to pupa (chrysalis) to adult (imago) — are called *metamorphosis*.

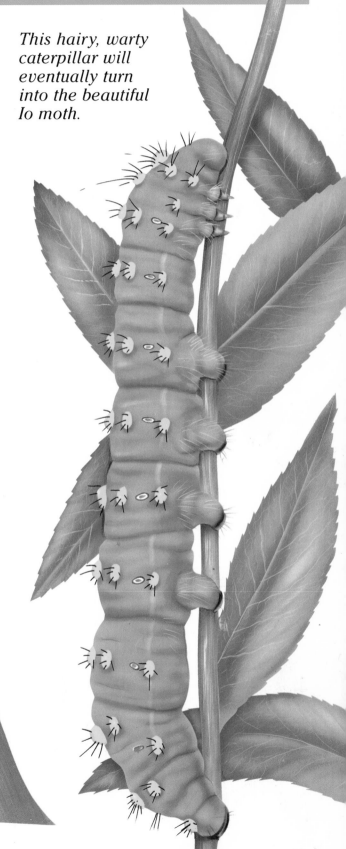

This hairy, warty caterpillar will eventually turn into the beautiful Io moth.

The caterpillars that emerge from these eggs will have plenty of food, since the eggs were laid on a food source.

Diurnal and nocturnal

Most butterflies are diurnal; they move around during daytime. Most moths, which also belong to the order Lepidoptera, are nocturnal; they move around mostly at night. It is easy to tell the difference between butterflies and moths. Diurnal butterflies flap their wings slowly and have smooth, club-shaped antennae. Moths have many different antennae shapes, but they are never smooth; they also beat their wings quickly. Moths have strong, hairy bodies that protect them from cold night weather. They also have narrow, pointed wings that fold into a covering. The tiger butterfly's bright colors tell other animals that it tastes

The shape of the butterfly depends on how it flies, how it defends itself against attack from enemies, and whether it is diurnal or nocturnal.

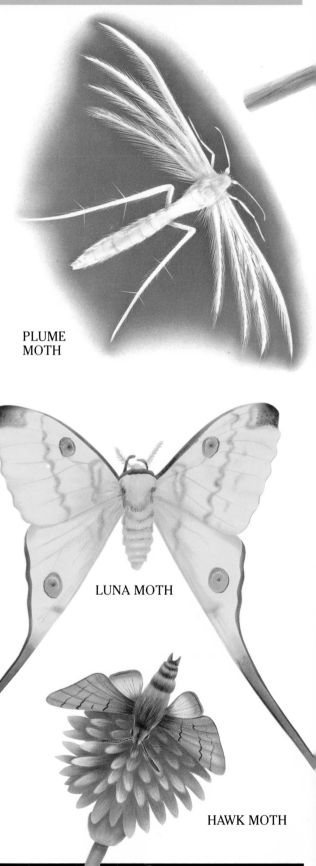

PLUME
MOTH

LUNA MOTH

HAWK MOTH

TIGER BUTTERFLY

HUMMINGBIRD MOTH

IO MOTH

horrible. The luna moth is beautiful but scarce. The plume moth has wings divided into what seem to be feathers, or plumes. The hawk moth is the fastest moth. The hummingbird moth can appear during the day; it looks a little like a bumblebee. The Io moth has circular wing designs that resemble the eyes of mammals. These designs provide natural camouflage.

Some butterflies measure only .08 inches (2 mm); others measure as much as 12 inches (30 cm).

THE BUTTERFLY'S METAMORPHOSIS

The butterfly's life cycle begins with an egg. A hungry larva, or caterpillar, comes out of the egg and eats the food that surrounds it. When the caterpillar has grown to its full size, it enters the pupa stage by changing into a chrysalis. Metamorphosis is complete when the butterfly emerges from its chrysalis. Adult butterflies appear during the spring. They sip nectar from the plants and help pollination.

COMPOUND EYES
Eyes are made up of thousands of small lenses. Each lens captures a part of the image and sends it to the brain. This helps the animal detect even small, rapid movements.

THE ADULT BUTTERFLY

ESOPHAGUS

ANTENNAE

BRAIN

DIGESTIVE SYSTEM
The chrysalis has a small digestive system because it hardly eats. The anus is not used and is reduced to just a little mark.

PROBOSCIS
The mouth of the adult butterfly, which can roll up or stretch out as much as 6 inches (15 cm) in some species.

FEMUR

HEART

THE CHRYSALIS

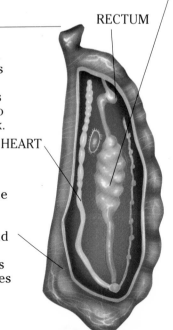

RECTUM

CREMASTER
Bottom part of the chrysalis abdomen. The chrysalis hangs upside-down; the cremaster has hairs and hooks it uses to hang on to the stalk.

HEART

SPIRACLES
Oxygen reaches the chrysalis through small air holes called spiracles and also through the blood. Caterpillars and adult butterflies have spiracles.

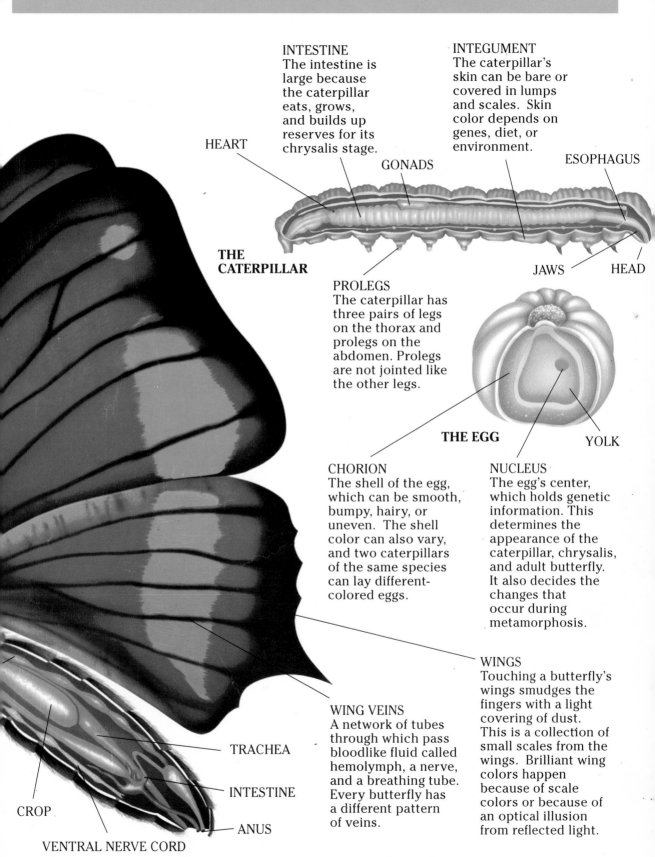

INTESTINE
The intestine is large because the caterpillar eats, grows, and builds up reserves for its chrysalis stage.

INTEGUMENT
The caterpillar's skin can be bare or covered in lumps and scales. Skin color depends on genes, diet, or environment.

HEART

GONADS

ESOPHAGUS

THE CATERPILLAR

JAWS

HEAD

PROLEGS
The caterpillar has three pairs of legs on the thorax and prolegs on the abdomen. Prolegs are not jointed like the other legs.

THE EGG

YOLK

CHORION
The shell of the egg, which can be smooth, bumpy, hairy, or uneven. The shell color can also vary, and two caterpillars of the same species can lay different-colored eggs.

NUCLEUS
The egg's center, which holds genetic information. This determines the appearance of the caterpillar, chrysalis, and adult butterfly. It also decides the changes that occur during metamorphosis.

WINGS
Touching a butterfly's wings smudges the fingers with a light covering of dust. This is a collection of small scales from the wings. Brilliant wing colors happen because of scale colors or because of an optical illusion from reflected light.

WING VEINS
A network of tubes through which pass bloodlike fluid called hemolymph, a nerve, and a breathing tube. Every butterfly has a different pattern of veins.

TRACHEA

INTESTINE

CROP

ANUS

VENTRAL NERVE CORD

FROM EGG TO PUPA

Laying eggs

The number of eggs a female butterfly lays depends on the species. Some butterflies lay as many as 4,000; others, only 100. The eggs can look different, too: bottle-shaped, round, or flat; black, white, gray, or red; smooth or uneven. The female usually lays its eggs on the backs of leaves, either in a string around the plant stalk or separately. The eggs usually take three to ten days to hatch, and then the caterpillars emerge. Sometimes the eggs or

The little caterpillar eats its nutritious shell when it emerges. This gives it strength to begin its rapid development.

caterpillars remain in the same stage over winter. This period of inactive time is called diapause.

Female butterflies can recognize which plants are best for their young. They have the sense of taste in their "feet" and in other parts of their bodies, such as the proboscis.

that there are
butterflies without wings?

Some female butterflies have wings that are so small they cannot fly; others do not have wings at all. These females look like the winged males of the species because they have antennae and legs, their bodies are scaly, and their senses are fully developed. An example of this is the beetlemoth. The adult female bagworm moth, however, has no wings, legs, mouth, or antennae. It looks more like an earthworm than the butterfly it really is.

The caterpillar and the mummy

The stage of metamorphosis after the egg is the larva, or caterpillar. The caterpillar has such a hearty appetite that it multiplies its weight 10,000 times before the pupa stage. Most caterpillars eat plants. Carpenter worm moth caterpillars, however, eat the wood inside oak trees. And wax moth caterpillars eat honeycombs. Caterpillars have a head, thorax, and abdomen. The jaws are in the head, along with the antennae and eyes. The thorax is the only part of the body that has jointed legs. The prolegs, which are not jointed like the those on the thorax, are located on the abdomen.

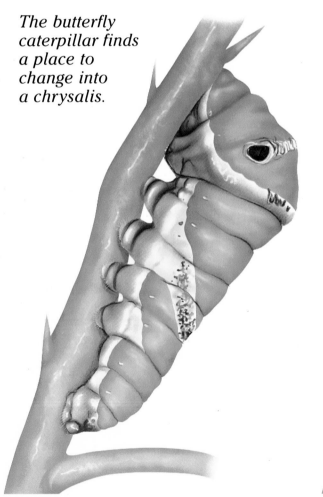

The butterfly caterpillar finds a place to change into a chrysalis.

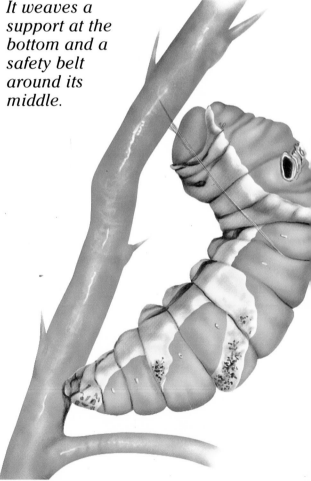

It weaves a support at the bottom and a safety belt around its middle.

A caterpillar cannot grow inside its protective covering, so it sheds its skin for a new, larger one. It changes its skin four or five times before the next stage, the pupa. During this stage, it appears to be wrapped in bandages, so some people call it a mummy.

Leaf-eating caterpillars move their heads up and down as they eat, leaving round bite marks on the leaf.

The caterpillar sheds its skin. Under it is the pupa, called a chrysalis.

The chrysalis can overwinter safely.

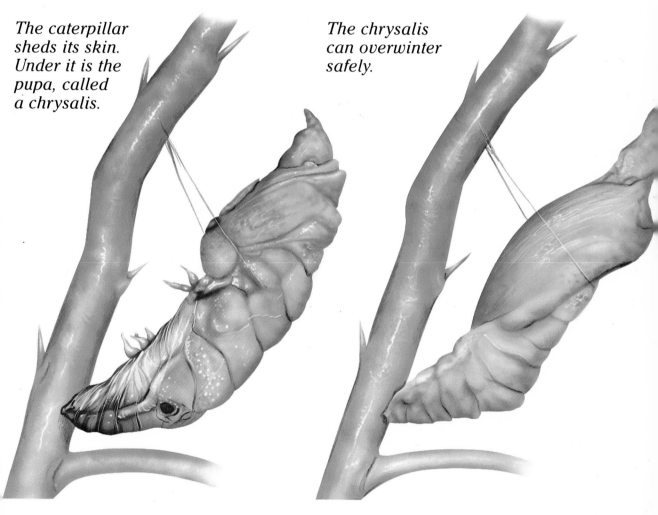

FROM PUPA TO ADULT

Chrysalis or cocoon

Although the butterfly pupa, or chrysalis, does not move, it is still alive. Inside, the pupa is changing into an adult butterfly.

A moth caterpillar spins a sturdy silk cocoon around itself, and then it becomes a pupa inside it. The moth pupa does not move either while it is changing into an adult moth.

Some moths sew leaves together to make a protective coat, and others bury themselves without any covering.

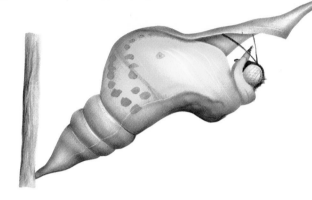

The wings, antennae, and abdominal parts of the adult butterfly appear just before it emerges.

To emerge from the strong silk cocoon, the adult moth cuts its way out with a sawlike comb on its head, or it softens the cocoon with a special liquid.

Left: Moths make silk cocoons starting with a single thread.

Far left: Butterflies use silk to secure the chrysalis.

that some butterflies don't eat?

Some butterflies live only a few hours, so they don't have much time for eating. They have to find a mate, and, if they are female, lay eggs. Some butterflies absorb nectar, and some drink the juices of flowers.

Others live on reserves accumulated during their time as caterpillars. Also, butterflies do not grow. The small amounts of food they eat replaces the energy they spend reproducing and flying.

Finally, a butterfly!

Metamorphosis is almost complete when the chrysalis turns into the adult butterfly. This is the only stage during which the insects can reproduce. Adults emerge from the chrysalis in spring, when the weather is good and plants are flowering. The adult breaks the chrysalis and begins to emerge, opening its wings. At this time, its abdomen is still swollen. To complete stretching and smoothing its wings, which are wrinkled, the butterfly injects hemolymph through the wing veins.

Like other animals after hibernation, the new butterfly quickly expels body wastes. The butterfly's waste is sometimes colored. In some cases, many adults emerge at once and expel

This magnified photo shows the structure of a butterfly's wings with its colored scales.

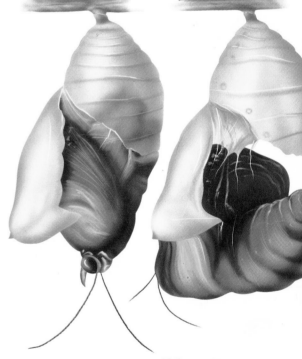

The butterfly breaks the chrysalis and uses its legs to push itself out.

When it emerges, the butterfly's body is soft. It waits for its body to harden and its wings to dry.

wastes at the same time, leaving red stains on the ground.

The adult butterfly's only task is to reproduce and leave descendants. Males die soon after mating; females die after laying their eggs.

The butterfly must extend its wings fully before they dry, or they might remain shorter than normal.

After opening and closing several times, the wings are dry, and the butterfly is ready for its first flight.

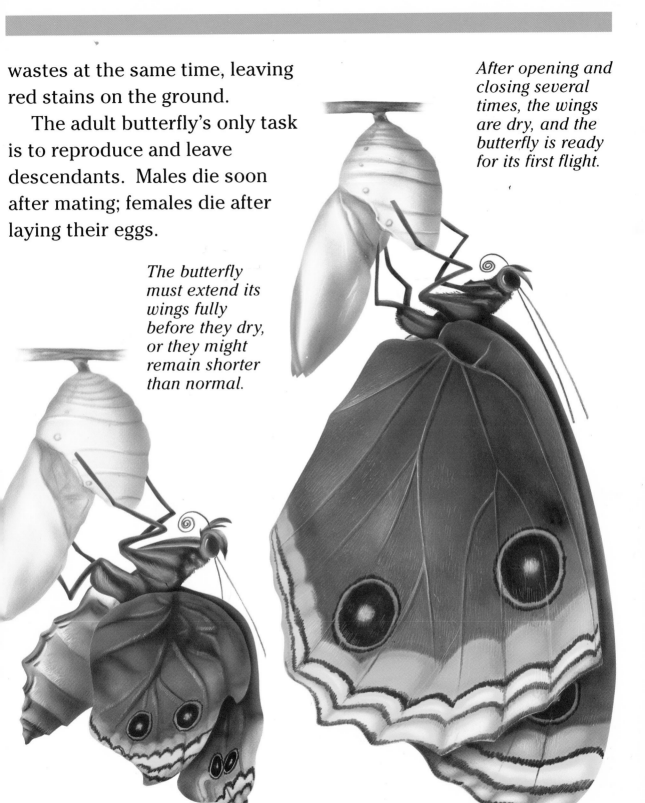

BUTTERFLY EVOLUTION

Butterflies and flowers

Only a few butterfly fossils have ever been discovered. The oldest remains are from 210 million years ago. These specimens had no proboscis, but they had jaws to chew pollen. Butterflies and flowers have evolved together to each others' benefit since flowering plants first appeared. Although the first butterflies damaged the plants because they ate the pollen, flowers later began to produce nectar to attract the butterflies. Over time, butterflies developed a suction tube. Along with other insects, they eventually became agents of pollination. By pollinating

Some butterflies sip nectar; others eat pollen like their ancestors.

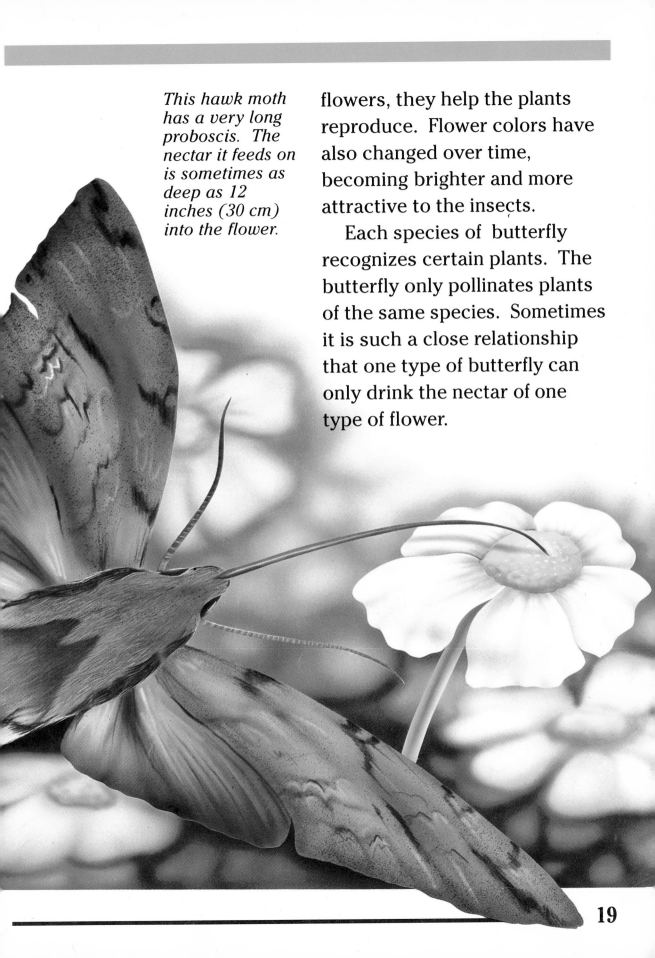

This hawk moth has a very long proboscis. The nectar it feeds on is sometimes as deep as 12 inches (30 cm) into the flower.

flowers, they help the plants reproduce. Flower colors have also changed over time, becoming brighter and more attractive to the insects.

Each species of butterfly recognizes certain plants. The butterfly only pollinates plants of the same species. Sometimes it is such a close relationship that one type of butterfly can only drink the nectar of one type of flower.

that there are moths with twenty-four wings?

The six-plumed moth has four wings divided into twenty-four parts that look like feathers. It lives in Europe and the cooler parts of North America. The larva lives either in a flower or inside the stem. Some species of the six-plumed moth live as adults for a whole year and survive the winter without any problem. There are 150 different species.

BUTTERFLY BEHAVIOR

Disarming deception

Each stage of the butterfly's development has a way of defending itself against predators. Its small size offers natural camouflage. Some caterpillars are protected by their prickly scales. They can also make threatening gestures, as in the case of the hawk moth. The bright, attractive colors of some butterflies warn their enemies, such as birds and lizards, that they have a terrible taste and are poisonous.

What a change! By swelling up the front part of its body, this caterpillar presents a menacing look.

These two butterflies may look alike, but they are two different species. One is poisonous, and the other is not. To be on the safe side, predators avoid both kinds.

The mating game

Butterflies and moths attract mates in different ways. Diurnal butterflies use their bright wing colors to attract partners. Nocturnal moths use their sense of smell to find their mates. With its antennae, a male moth detects the odor of a substance produced by the female. The female moth secretes this male-attracting substance while looking for a place to lay eggs. This way, she doesn't waste valuable time searching for a male first.

Many male moths have hairy antennae that can detect the distinctive aroma of the females.

Male and female butterflies can stay coupled while flying.

The silkworm moth

For thousands of years, the Chinese people have raised silkworms in order to use the silk thread from their cocoons. A newly-hatched silkworm is fed mulberry leaves for about seven weeks. Then it spins a silk cocoon and turns into a pupa. The silk growers kill most of the pupae with heat, and the valuable cocoon thread is carefully unwound to be made into silk fabric. Some pupae are

Inside the cocoon, the silkworm forms the pupa from which the silkworm moth will emerge.

allowed to finish growing into moths; these destroy their cocoons when they emerge. A broken cocoon cannot be used.

The silkworm moth emerges from a cocoon made from one silk thread 1 mile (1.6 km) long.

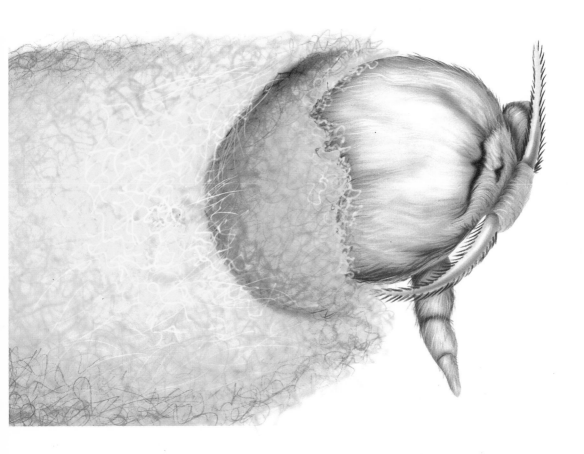

APPENDIX TO

SECRETS
OF THE
ANIMAL WORLD

BUTTERFLIES
Magical Metamorphosis

BUTTERFLY SECRETS

▼ **Unusual models.** Many butterflies have colors and markings on their wings that work as camouflage.

▼ **Parasite wasps.** Females of some wasp species perforate the skin of a caterpillar and lay their eggs inside. Larvae emerge and feed on the tissue of the caterpillar. They

eventually move outward and form a pupa on top of the caterpillar. The caterpillar cannot survive this invasion and dies before it can make a pupa of its own.

▼ **Noisy moths.** When the death's head moth senses danger, it makes a chirping sound to frighten its enemies. When it goes into beehives to steal honey, it makes a sound that imitates the queen bee to deceive the workers.

Migration. Some butterflies migrate in winter to warmer weather. The monarch butterfly, for example, travels 1,864 miles (3,000 km) from the northern United States to Mexico.

Carnivorous worms. Some caterpillars feed on ant larvae. In exchange, the ants get a syrup the caterpillar produces. The caterpillar forms a pupa inside the anthill, and the butterfly or moth emerges through its passages.

▶ **Crafty caterpillars.** The hairy caterpillars of moths in the Notodontidae family can cause a great deal of plant damage. Known as processionary caterpillars, these larvae live in communal webs and march in columns to their food source. Each larva lays down a silken thread as it moves along. The caterpillars return to their original place by following the threads left as a trail.

1. Diapause refers to . . .
a) a period of high activity.
b) the colored wastes of moths.
c) a period of rest or inactivity.

2. Why do some butterflies have bright colors?
a) To warn predators they are poisonous.
b) To attract prey.
c) To look like the flowers they drink from.

3. Caterpillars . . .
a) have a proboscis.
b) do not eat.
c) have jaws for chewing.

4. The butterfly . . .
a) folds its wings to make a roof.
b) has smooth, club-shaped antennae.
c) buzzes as it flies.

5. What emerges from a butterfly's egg?
a) A caterpillar.
b) A chrysalis.
c) An adult butterfly.

6. Which moth do humans raise in great numbers?
a) The processionary moth.
b) The silkworm moth.
c) The skull's head moth.

The answers to BUTTERFLY SECRETS questions are on page 32.

GLOSSARY

absorb: to soak up, or take in, a substance. Some butterflies absorb nectar from flowers.

camouflage: to disguise someone or something to make it look like its surroundings. Butterflies and moths often have natural color camouflage to help them blend in with their habitat and stay safe from predators.

chrysalis: the hard, shiny, and often brightly-colored pupa of a butterfly during its third, inactive stage of growth.

cocoon: a strong, silky covering that a moth caterpillar spins around itself for protection while it turns into a pupa during its third, inactive stage of growth.

diurnal: active during the daytime hours.

emerge: to appear or come out of something. An adult butterfly emerges from a chrysalis.

esophagus: a muscular tube that connects the throat and the stomach.

evolution: the process of changing shape or developing gradually over time. All living things change and adapt to survive or they can become extinct. Most of today's life-forms, including humans, evolved from ancestors that may have looked and behaved quite differently. Scientists learn more about how organisms develop by studying how they once were or what their ancestors were like through fossils.

fossils: the remains of an animal or plant from an earlier time period that are often found in rock or in Earth's crust.

habitat: the natural home of a plant or animal.

hemolymph: a colorless, bloodlike substance that moves through the butterfly's circulatory system and the veins in its wings. Hemolymph is common in all invertebrates (animals without backbones).

hibernation: a state of inactivity in which most body functions, such as heartbeat and breathing, slow down for a while.

honeycomb: a structure of hexagonal (six-sided) wax cells built by bees in their hives. The bees store pollen, honey, and eggs in the honeycomb.

integument: a protective layer, or covering. A caterpillar's skin, or integument, can be smooth and bare or covered with lumps and scales.

Lepidoptera: the scientific order of insects that includes butterflies and moths. Insects in this order have millions of tiny scales covering their wings and body. Together, these scales make different patterns, often in brilliant colors.

metamorphosis: a complete change in form or appearance; metamorphosis often occurs in different stages. For example, the four stages in a butterfly's life cycle include the egg, larva (caterpillar), pupa (chrysalis), and adult (imago). This series of changes is called metamorphosis.

moths: flying insects related to butterflies that also belong to the scientific order Lepidoptera.

Moths differ from butterflies in that they have plumper bodies, duller coloring, smaller wings, and feathery antennae. Most moths are also nocturnal, or active at night, while most butterflies are diurnal, or active during the day.

nectar: a sweet liquid found in many flowers that is often used as a food source by insects. Most butterflies sip nectar with their proboscis. During this feeding process, they often gather pollen without realizing it and then carry the pollen to other flowers they visit. In this way, the butterflies become agents of pollination.

nocturnal: active at night. Moths are nocturnal insects.

pollinate: to carry pollen (tiny yellow grains that form a fine dust) to the part of a flower called the stigma so that it can produce fruit or seeds. Many insects pollinate plants without realizing it as they search for nectar to eat.

predators: animals that hunt and kill other animals for food.

proboscis: the long feeding tube, or tongue, located on or under the head of some insects. The butterfly uncoils its proboscis, which is located on the front of its head, to search for nectar inside flowers.

pupa: the third, inactive stage of growth (metamorphosis) of a moth or butterfly, while it is changing from a caterpillar into an adult insect. Pupae have a hard, shell-like covering made from chitin, a horny material.

species: a group of closely-related animals or plants that are often similar in behavior and appearance. Members of the same species can breed together.

thorax: the middle segment of an insect's three major body parts. The butterfly and moth thorax contains two pairs of wings and three pairs of legs.

veins: in butterflies and moths, narrow tubes that form the framework of the wings.

ACTIVITIES

◆ Find out which species of butterflies and moths are native to your area. Then do some research to find out what humans have been doing to threaten these insects, and also what you can do to encourage the insects to stay around and pollinate flowers and crops. Many types of flowering plants, for example, can attract certain types of butterflies. Make a plan to plant some.

◆ Go to your local library and research the migratory habits of the beautiful monarch butterflies. Where do they live during summer, and where do they make their home in winter? Do they always return to the same places when they migrate? How many travel together at once? If it is summer, or if you live in a warm part of the country, stay up some night after dark and put up a bright light bulb somewhere outside where you can sit nearby. How many kinds of moths and other nocturnal insects are drawn to the light? You may be surprised at how large some of the moths can be!

MORE BOOKS TO READ

Amazing Insects. (Running Press)
Butterfly and Moth. Paul Whalley (Knopf)
A Day in the Life of the Monarch Butterfly. Liz Zappler (Sunbelt Media)
Exploring the World of Insects: The Equinox Guide to Insect Behavior.
   Adrian Forsyth (Firefly Books)
Eyewitness Explorers: Insects. (Dorling Kindersley)
The Fascinating World of Butterflies and Moths. M. A. Julivert (Barron)
Insect Metamorphosis: From Egg to Adult. R. and N. Goor (Macmillan)
Invisible Bugs and Other Creepy Creatures That Live With You.
   Susan S. Lang (Sterling)
The Monarch Butterfly. Judith P. Josephson (Macmillan)
The Moon of the Monarch Butterflies. Jean C. George (HarperCollins)

VIDEOS

Butterflies. (MNTEX Entertainment)
Butterfly: The Monarch's Life Cycle. (International Film Bureau)
Insects: The Little Things That Run the World. (Smithsonian Institution)

PLACES TO VISIT

**The Field Museum of
   Natural History**
Roosevelt Road at Lake
   Shore Drive
Chicago, IL 60605

**Otto Orkin Insect Zoo
   National Museum of
   Natural History
   The Smithsonian
   Institution**
10 Constitution Avenue
Washington, D.C. 20560

**Butterfly House, in
   Royal Melbourne
   Zoological Gardens**
Elliott Avenue
Parkville, Victoria
Australia 3052

**Auckland Zoological
   Park**
Motions Road
Western Springs
Auckland 2
New Zealand

**Calgary Zoo, Botanical
   Garden, and
   Prehistoric Park**
1300 Zoo Road
Calgary, Alberta
T2E 7V6

**Metropolitan Toronto
   Zoo**
Meadowvale Road
   West Hill
Toronto, Ontario
M1E 4R5

INDEX

Answers to BUTTERFLY SECRETS questions:

1. c
2. a
3. c
4. b
5. a
6. b